THE PACIFIC NORTHWEST POETRY SERIES

Linda Bierds, General Editor

THE PACIFIC NORTHWEST POETRY SERIES

P O S T
R O M A N T I C

POEMS BY **KATHLEEN FLENNIKEN**

UNIVERSITY OF WASHINGTON PRESS

Seattle

Post Romantic, the twenty-first volume in the Pacific Northwest Poetry Series, is published with the generous support of Cynthia Lovelace Sears.

Design by Katrina Noble
Composed in Scala, typeface designed by Martin Majoor

24 23 22 21 20   5 4 3 2 1

Printed and bound in the United States of America

UNIVERSITY OF WASHINGTON PRESS
uwapress.uw.edu

LIBRARY OF CONGRESS CATALOGING-IN-PUBLICATION DATA
Names: Flenniken, Kathleen, author.
Title: Post romantic / poems by Kathleen Flenniken.
Description: Seattle : University of Washington Press, [2020] | Series: Pacific
    Northwest poetry series
Identifiers: LCCN 2020015466 (print) | LCCN 2020015467 (ebook) | ISBN
    9780295747798 (hardcover : acid-free paper) | ISBN 9780295748405
    (ebook)
Subjects: LCGFT: Poetry.
Classification: LCC PS3606.L47 P67 2020 (print) | LCC PS3606.L47 (ebook) |
    DDC 811/.6—dc23
LC record available at https://lccn.loc.gov/2020015466
LC ebook record available at https://lccn.loc.gov/2020015467

The paper used in this publication is acid free and meets the minimum requirements of American National Standard for Information Sciences—Permanence of Paper for Printed Library Materials, ANSI Z39.48–1984.∞

for Steve

Isn't it time
that our loving freed us from the one we love?

—RAINER MARIA RILKE, *DUINO ELEGIES*

CONTENTS

POST ROMANTIC

INSTEAD OF SHEEP

try counting down years
of the 20th century

nothing frightening at first   just
miniatures in a glass case

etched with your name
'99 the Hogwarts sand castle

'90 the garnet earrings
hanging like grapes

counting down your life
with prayer beads

'84 the summer night in the new car
with a new red wine stain

waiting for a morning ferry
'68 the assassinations of RFK and MLK

each year has its feel
just like mathematicians say

of prime numbers
a purple fuzziness or sunrise glow

you've outrun
your own lived years

it doesn't hurt much to be carried
back   tiny   like change in a purse

by silvery images

like the one fluttering from the burn pile
in the winter after Mother and Dad died

their '47 wedding portrait
under a dusty film   both grandfathers

strangers   already looking frail
you should be asleep by now

the war's furnaces and bombs
when you were trapped in French class '77

watching the freeing of Auschwitz '45
skulls with eyes   Hiroshima   Nagasaki

'43 Dad in uniform
your parents grow childish and wispy

but history runs strong
'28 speakeasies and chuckling tommy guns

you're carried close like a pretty watch
pinned to your grandmother's belt

clouds whisper and uncurl
as she waves to a backward-sailing ship

a chuffing train
a river as glassy and black as obsidian

through the trees   to a trail
engraved

by ashes swept   aloft

LETTER TO RILKE

November 2016

I'm remembering a western scene. I was a child
sticky hot between my brothers
in the backseat of a Buick doing 80

down a two-lane highway. The desert gaped
like the shed shell of some giant writhing thing.
The truth was just as alien—

basalt plateaus and canyons carved
15,000 years ago by cataclysmic floods.
But the floods were still an arcane discredited

theory. And because we didn't know,
we couldn't see. We skittered across
the massive landscape completely ignorant,

inhaling my father's cigar smoke.

○ ○

Viewed from that line of pelicans flying,
our car crawled like an ant in a trail of ants
following the river—

though the river was so systematically
dammed, it was by then a series of still lakes.
From my place in the backseat

I watched my mother in sunglasses
glance at my father, glance at my brothers
and me, then back to the highway

with a look I took for granted then,
but don't now that I'm older. You wrote
that angels and animals are complete,

but we humans are made of lack
and what we're striving for *was once nearer*
and truer and attached to us with infinite tenderness.

And so I'm drawn again to that moment in the car
by Mother's expression—content.
Whole for a moment. Holy.

o o

Your angels muscle through the now and then
and what's to come, not caring
where they plant their feet. Not caring

who they crush. So stainless and complete.
They look down on us, stopping 50 years ago
for gas, more cigars, and Eskimo Pies

and on the man behind us in line.
He needed cigarettes. His nails were clean
but his hands worse for wear

and he looked older then
than a man his age now. Like every man
in that filling station, he'd gone to war.

Out back in a patch of weeds
we swung our feet at a picnic table,
slapped mosquitoes, bit into ice cream

and licked our wrists
while the man behind us lit up,
gunned his American engine and drove on.

o   o

Motel postcards showed a bowl of sky
tinged with green—a generous cocktail
of leaded gas and low-level radiation.

To you this is America's future,
a star sapphire, a weird and worldly blue
with a burst of light inside,

but to me it's an irretrievable past.
The man in his car was the best of us.
That's almost true. He populated this nation—

decent, hardworking; you'd say *his streaming*
godhead inciting the night to infinite uproar.
His godhead by day only nudging the surface.

Head cocked, hat, shoulders back.
He'd been a soldier. Killing men brought no relief
and he never spoke of it.

America has always been defined
by haunted men and women,
but this one bore an extra burden—

our newfound power to kill everything.

o o

I remember a motel I always looked for
pitched on the bluff over a hydroelectric dam—
centipedal warrens each with closed drapes

and orange doors. Transmission towers
marched up the hills through the sagebrush,
and the dam was lit at night like a prison.

Along with that neon sign—MOTEL—
it was the only consequential light in town.
The drapes stayed closed.

I'm trying to marry then and now:
Dear Rilke,
I enter one of those rooms,

slide in beside the man and see him
no better for our nakedness.
How uneasily I love America.

o o

An everyman / bystander / scapegoat / citizen /
racist / chosen one / extra / blur at the edge
of the frame / peripheral man. I studied him

in the hardware store where he studied
the penny nails. I studied him on the highway,
his hands at ten and two.

I studied him on the news,
blasted by a fire hose, or standing back
to watch it happen, or bracing the hose

as it blasted away. I studied him
on the convention floor with fellow delegates,
or fellow strikers. Aiding or aiming

in a National Guard uniform.
On a stool in a diner, drinking coffee alone.
From the low angle of a child.

That man is gone now.
If I call to him, he isn't here to answer.
He is what's missing.

o o

Your angels don't distinguish time.
They see us all, dead and alive and yet to be,
tracing the river highway together.

They see me with my old America,
behind pulled drapes.
They hear him in my ear, despairing

for the wreck of it we've made,
though even in the throes of nostalgia,
I never quite believe in his goodness.

It's a running argument in my head.
Good at fixing broken flashlights
and tumbling rocks in the garage.

Good at keeping violent visions private.
Good at separating needs from wants.
He wraps me up and I'm safe

in my bare brown hills. *Look at me,*
he commands, but he's too close.
I shut my eyes and say *I am.*

○ ○

Then open them. We fall and rise and fall—
strange, then familiar, then strange.
Stupid, intolerant, and greedy,

then a little better, then backward again
because we never learn.
Angels gesture toward our screens:

barkers barking in a sideshow—
how money breeds! money's genitals! everything,
the whole act! Barkers are running for president.

America is nearly gone,
with the man who sold us ice cream
and the man in line.

I mistook the gold landscape
for a golden age. Mother's eyes
remain half hidden behind dark glass—

it was the child in me
that only saw the sunlit half.
Rilke, you helped me see the present clearly—

dogs doing their business,
sideshow carnies and the carnival crowd,
and one pair of lovers in the grass.

One pair of lovers to love for all of us.
What is there to do but stare so hard I feel his lips
on her lips, his palm on her blossoming breast

and wish myself between them.

TO DOTTED LINES

that instruct
where to
fold
paper hearts,
cut tabs
on Betsy McCall's
skirt and ice skates,
walk
from Patient Intake to
Emergency Room A.

Shortcut
for your pawn
rounding the
Huckleberry Hound
gameboard.

Dividing
lanes
and states.
Demarking
theoretical
landings for
bank robbers
in parachutes,
hundred-year floods,
nuclear fallout.

Asymptotes
at o and π.
Maximum volume,

minimum height,
finish line.

The detectible
connection
between a wife
and somebody else's
husband.

Warning you
in urgent Morse code—
dash, dash, dash.
Oh, oh, oh—

zones
vulnerable
to touch.
Before-
and after-
silhouettes
of love.

Trajectory
of a bullet
before
the trigger's pulled.
Outline
of a body
where it lay.

Awaiting
your signature,
scissors,
dancing feet.

Denoting
whispers,
caught breath.

Ghost map
of your grave.

ON THIS DAY IN HISTORY

*. . .Charles Lindbergh, Jr. was discovered dead beside a road, buried in dirt
and leaves.*

I find a small body
in a doctor's office magazine
and the shadow

of an inconsolable nanny
waiting for my tea water to boil.
Once in Tacoma

I stared at a torn yellow window-shade
four stories above the street
and felt on its other side

a drifter working the kinks
out of a famous kidnapping scheme.
It was the light,

which is bound up in my theory
of time travel, which is tied to the angle
and intensity of the sun—

the diffuse light emitted in a stand
of woods, the smoky light
inside a falling-down barn.

I'm stepping through
black and white woods,
then plunged into green. Here,

after months, under a fallen limb—
the last thing I said that I still mean.
Compare its grain of truth

to the ladder leaning
against the Lindbergh window.
I've stumbled on my father

and his twin in their baby buggy
riding shafts
of early 20th-century sun

and my own unformed self
in the shade of a 1960s tasseled awning.
Time is a poor alibi

and there are too many coincidences
to explain—the baby's headstone
engraved with my birth date,

my instinct for escape,
this lifelong fascination
with flying.

STREET SCENE, 1964

A little girl sprawls on the living-room rug,
pushing a matchbox car and ambulance
along a make-believe street.
She reenacts the scene out her window—
car, stretcher, woman standing by
who could be mother or driver, and child.

o o

The matchbox car is so convincing
she can't help but peer inside.
Its empty seats are freshly disappointing.
As though the driver has fled
to check the child for a heartbeat,
or stand by useless
as a statue.

o o

The little girl playing on her knees
hears brakes from the street
and cleanses the scene
of anything but little plastic people.

You could buy them
by the dozen in cellophane bags.
The postman holding mail,
mechanic with an oil can,
four firemen wielding axes.

o o

There's something out there
she can't comprehend.
Her mother pulls her gently from the window
and asks about the street on the rug
and what about the cars
and where are all the little people going?

KARAOKE

Do something, you're his wife! somebody begs me

when you're a couple of verses in
but wasn't everybody forced to take a turn?

I watch you center stage where you never ever
want to be, stunned in the revolving red lights

of Jimi Hendrix, "Are You Experienced?"
a song we now know has no melody or end.

Laughing is wrong. What else is there?
Your boss records the crime on his iPhone.

It's suddenly clear how much effort
goes into just being, just holding ourselves still,

our bizarre niceties and party-store leis,
the saucy meatball you stabbed

then abandoned on a plastic plate.
A few with good manners pay no attention

and pore over the list of has-been anthems.
How did we get this far into a foreign century,

this many levels down into middle age?
Outside the bar it's night.

We've got to find our car in the frigging cold
and make conversation all the way home.

I won't be able to say I wanted to wrap you
in a blanket like the survivor of a five-alarm fire,

and who cares if you were naked?

MARRIED LOVE

All of them are dead now.
My father and mother, bedded together

under their matching stones.
Their married friends, close by.

The crystal and good plates all washed
and put away in other homes,

no party food left over. My job
was to whip the cream for dessert

and ride behind on their fishing weekends
like a seventh wheel,

along with our Airedale who wore
striped socks over his muddy paws

in the house. Spirits accelerated
toward cocktail hour in the red

ranch kitchen where they made
big to-dos over their drinks—

then feigned concern they might
corrupt me. The men stirred

the air, clustered at the bar, moved
among the women conferring

over the bubbling stew.
My mother, flushed and pretty

as a cornucopia of summer fruit.
That September before college

I joined the happy group
on a fly-fishing river in Montana

and slept on the cottage's foldout couch.
Late one evening, lights doused,

I was alone with Mother and one
of the men, not quite uncle

not quite friend though I newly
recognized that he was handsome.

I've erased whatever he said
that convinced me he'd forgotten

I was there. But there I was, afraid
to breathe, confused to learn

how delicately balanced
these practitioners of marriage must be.

Then they retired to their separate rooms,
though a presence hung in the air

like perfume.

STORY THAT WON'T END WELL

It begins in a laboratory
under a football field.

While the Axis rolls
over distant continents,

50,000 nomads
journey to the American West

to construct cathedrals in the desert
for Nobel physicists,

performing feats
they're not privileged to understand

to microscopic tolerances
in dust storms the stuff of legend.

Periscopes and code words,
train cars loaded with uranium,

the heroism of a just war—
all prologue to the story

we can't see, smell, or taste,
that seeps underground

and drifts undetected
downstream and downwind,

while the Soviets match us
bomb for bomb,

while we build lives
and more reactors, pledge

allegiance, defend the key,
plant birches in the yard

and a Naugahyde couch
in the family room.

Our story develops
invisibly, incrementally,

until one afternoon
it daylights in town square

and we force ourselves to *read it*
bubbling there—

the ugly, stinking, bitter truth.

And some fall down.
And some go home, unmoved.

OUR FATHERS

owned the atomic age. They were young and handsome
in their bow ties, courting the Cold War and principles of fission,
    the absolute of a scientific solution.

Shaved and shined, sporting bright wives and bonny children,
grinding out reports and chain smoking,
    our fathers owned the atom and were young and handsome
    in their bow ties boarding planes for Washington.

Bridge club, cocktails, school board meetings,
whole-body counts, contamination, secret-keeping—
    owned them, aged but never changed them
    in their bow ties. Even dying,
    trusting Science to save them. It betrayed them.

A CHILD'S BOOK OF AMERICA

By the time I could read
its title—*My Prayers*—

I'd already learned religion
from my favorite illustration inside—

a blond girl gazing from a hilltop
at her American town below.

American because of the white church
and wide streets. And because

under the gabled roofs
the artist implied garden rakes

and comfortable rooms pungent
with furniture wax and clocks

that chimed, and in the kitchen,
butter on a dish, and in the closet

a button jar and dozens of bright
spools of thread. I resolved

to be just the same—blond,
with a clock in the hall and a father

who came home to dinner
served in clouds of steam.

I learned America is a religion
and praying feels like envy.

The spirit has moved me again and again.

1968

That year we liked our ranks,
our neat columns and rows of desks,
or didn't know not to, we girls
in plaid and sashes, we boys
with pocket slingshots,

turning to our reading in classrooms
circumscribed by shoebox dioramas
and the number line, we boys
running in recess packs, we girls
collecting hopscotch chains,

who fogged the small-paned windows
on orange afternoons
to write our names, then
a birthday party after school, a pinwheel
thumb-tacked on a pencil to take home,

and rarely, maybe only once that year,
someone brought a coconut to share,
say a souvenir of David G.'s uncle's
trip across an ocean—

a hairy husk hammered open,
woody crescents divvied up,
oily milk from a Dixie-cup—

though we didn't like the taste
and we complained
as the world began impinging
on our world with its satellites,
its news reports, and something in us knew

it shouldn't, yet. Because it was enough
to lie in the dark and wait for sleep,

we girls decoding voices
from another room, we boys
alert for squealing tires and police.

THE LAKE

The frogs are singing
and the moonlit street is silver

like a magically detailed rendering
on my childhood Etch-A-Sketch

though I don't remember etching anything
but stairs and little peepholes

to try and figure out how the whole thing
worked. Maybe that's what I should do—

get out of bed and rub away the scene
to peek at the master mechanism

behind frogs, April, shy sleep.
Though hasn't opacity

always been my friend? Haven't I said,
I wouldn't dare . . .

and followed that up with nothing?
The world tonight is dipped

in silver. I'm twisting left and right
against the frogs' wild songs,

against the still and silver lake.

I won't get up.
Not even to open the window.

Someone else break the surface
and tell me what's below.

NIGHT TRAIN FROM SALZBURG

It was over 30 years ago. The middle leg
of our six-week European tour.
I forgive you for remembering Salzburg,
then the Jungfrau in Switzerland, but nothing
of how we traveled from one to the other.

It was midnight. We'd reserved two couchettes
in a second-class compartment.
The conductor lectured us severely,
we didn't understand a word, then slipped
into a dark room humid with sleeping.
Our eyes adjusted to the window light.
One empty top bunk, one middle.
The rest occupied. The rest

my private discovery. A crisp Germanic sheet,
one blanket, one pillow. The impression of you
invisible in the bunk above me, settling yourself
and your pack. Four strangers' rhythmic breathing,
like four tangled silver chains I worked to separate.
Our train pulling away from the station.

Then your breath braided in. I slept fitfully,
surrounded by slumbering as we threaded along
the Alps. *Giddum giddum. Giddum giddum.*
I imagined the train tracing the contours
of a charming relief map punctuated
with wiener schnitzel, tidy geraniums in window boxes,
felt hats, and precision folding knives.
Finally the scene outside began to lighten
and I could discern occasional smudges transforming

into Swiss chalets, dark dots which became, much later,
sweet brown cows with bells around their necks.

Giddum giddum. Giddum giddum. The wayfarer's
perfect lullaby. The mountains lightened
from grey into green. Deep in a high valley.
As though we'd been dropped into a diorama
or a View-Master stereoscopic slide.

And for that while, not dark, not light,
as I floated between my life and what it might become,
you slept and kept sleeping, you were part of the others
with their easy breathing, not part of me.

o   o

Long marriage is predicted by patterns
of call and response.
One sees a goldfinch out the window and comments.
The other responds with an interested, *Oh!*
One suggests an article in the newspaper
and the other is pleased because she missed it,
and says so. Not passion, the experts say.
Not probing each other's depths.
Just human birdsong.

o   o

Today you said it rained on your bike ride home
and I asked if your old jacket kept you dry.
I was thinking in the back of my mind
it might be a thoughtful present for your birthday.
Then I looked up. You were wet to the skin
and drenching the kitchen floor.

o o

Giddum giddum. Giddum giddum. Giddum giddum.
When the cabin lightened enough,
my eyes made out the bunks,
then finally the sleepers.
A stranger lay next to me,
and each silver breath taken was a link
that tugged me closer, close enough
to touch, intimate and strange at once.
Memory erased was it man or woman,
old or young? Just a someone. And yet
that sleeping figure under a blanket
occupies a treasured place
in my story of our courtship.
And if I don't know why,
I'll keep remembering until I puzzle it out.

o o

On our last day in Salzburg
we'd both been out of sorts.
Too much togetherness, perhaps,
and the weight of knowing this long trip
was a dry run for a life together.
If it went well. And so we'd squabbled
all afternoon. We sat on a bench
overlooking the Salzach River. The rest
is a blank except Mozarteum Hall
which I remember as lemon yellow
ornamented with white meringue,
chamber music as warm as varnished
scrollwork, and something
in the glittering space above my head—

a meeting of question marks
that had trailed me for days.

○ ○

We can both recall meals we shared
more than half our lives ago.
Thinly sliced salmon in Avignon.
The black, black gravy in a cassoulet.
Our midnight supper on the Left Bank—
not what we ate, but that customers
kept piling in, in the middle of the night!
Even as we were leaving!
The prawns in Soho.
Our morning option in North England
of orange juice *or* corn flakes.
And the couple in Polperro who served us
and thanked us as they lay each course down,
which prompted us to thank them, which
prompted them to thank us for thanking them.

○ ○

When a marriage partner dies or leaves,
how do you calculate the loss?
Beyond the familiar voice, habit,
shared chores, the other's body
to scent and warm the bed, rhythms
of mood, a pattern of likes and concerns,
of tuna fish and birthday cake requests,
a certain quality of junk in the junk drawer.
Coaxing the garden into compliance.
An attitude with a hand saw.
The mouth sounds of frustration. Or boredom.
A texture to his thinning hair. His capable

and beautiful hands, his memory of my parents
who are gone. Our tiny babies in his arms.

The great loss is the other's memories of your past.
Your better half who sometimes remembered
what you forgot.

o o

I call to you as I'm preparing our dinner
but you're lost in that vague state
that passes as hard of hearing
but is more like traveling alone
through an abstracted landscape
of horizon and careful brushwork.

o o

There was that extra hour after the world
seemed fully light. Still you all kept sleeping
as I watched the Alpine postcards rushing by,
beautiful clichés, impossibly green meadows
dotted with blooms, but at each charming chalet,
I sensed complicated inner lives.

Then the conductor saved me with a knock
and woke us all and turned our beds into seats.
The six of us returned to our compartment,
exhausted, and tried not to stare at each other.

o o

Six months later you proposed
and confessed you'd meant to ask
that afternoon in Salzburg

on the bench by the river
where we argued instead.

o o

That figure in the couchette beside me
that I can't remember and can't forget?
It was possibly me in some parallel life
sleeping easily with her different decisions.
Or it was someone I'll never meet—
as much or as little as that means.
In any case I walked off the train with you,
both of us hauling our heavy packs
full of trinkets to take home
and torn maps of foreign countries.

ESTRANGED

from Old French estranger, *from Late Latin* extrāneāre, *to treat as a stranger*

So much sadness in two syllables.
To say it, to be mid-saying it,

is to enter from a sunny antechamber
into a corridor of portraits
once dear, now defaced,
hard to look at straight on,

where I linger
(because time stretches inside some words)
studying my past
for clues or any other way out.

Then it's said and done.
I'm unsure what waits
on the other side of its latch
beyond the silence

that registers at the edges
like stars.

ANDY WARHOL, 1986

Robert Mapplethorpe

A face is just an arrangement of holes.
You've plugged the light in yours. Eyes stare out but
business stays closed. Your mien is oatmeal
served over amphetamines and steel.
Your nostrils are private entrances
where security guards poke flashlights
at doped-up actresses. Your dark brows brood
like austere hilltop factories belching
Brillo pads, Trojans, and General Foods
for the masses like me to consume.
Your ears are police scanners tuning in death.
Your mouth's a sign on a famous discotheque.
It reads, lips not moving, *Not you. Not ever.*
You're boring, and boredom spells terror.

A CHILDHOOD FEAR OF GEORGES BRAQUE

She confused the art book on the living room table
with daily headlines shouting SOVIET UNION—,

conflated Braque's masterpiece, *Man with a Guitar,*
and the TV newscaster's phrase, *the Iron Curtain.*

The bricked and mortared "man" on the page
somehow conveyed without hands, or mouth,

or guitar, the rat-a-tat of a radio bulletin.
The painting's industrial grays, browns, and black,

and menacing light from above,
the unnerving expression of every side at once—

collided with the postatomic world.
She memorized its page number.

If it's true the young have ignorance to shield them,
then for a while she could hide

from men on TV ducking into black sedans,
missile counts, and newspapers crawling with words.

The image in Plate 13 didn't ask her to understand.
It asked only for fear.

THE JET AGE

Behind the airport, two boys
sit on a homemade raft

on a black pond scummed
with jet oil.

Game shows and soap operas
leak from the neighbors'

cracked windows.
Planes take off

with a rhythmic roar.
One boy is only four—

he will be my husband.
The other is twelve

and famous in the neighborhood
as slow.

Now my husband's mother
pulls up in the family sedan,

coaxes the boys back to the bank
and drives her lucky son home.

Do you see the slow boy
beached on his rickety raft?

Next week he will drown
in those concentric circles

of airplane fuel.
It's foretold in the waste plumes

written on the sky
and in the ripples

we'll call a sinking stone.
You can see it

if you know where to look—
a scream

caught in the edges
of then and now.

1973

My father invited a Black man to dinner
the year I turned thirteen. My parents had only just stopped
saying "Negro." I loved him for the idea, I was mortified
on the man's behalf, and set the table for four

North East South West

with our suddenly embarrassing china and sterling silverware
while in the kitchen Mother prepared her stuffed green peppers
as if they were the choice of Black men everywhere
though she kept asking, Do you think he'll like this?

My father arrived with our Black guest

a visiting scientist bearing a soft Tennessee accent.
He shook our hands and I didn't die.
Dad pressed him with a drink and whether or not he drank
he made a gracious toast. We all smiled

and sat down together, each taking a side

as if to play cards, or call up the dead
and though I finally had to exhale and blink
the evening hovered delicately over our peppers
of its own accord. I thought that night

he was the bravest man in the world.

He sent two green vases shaped like peppers.
They graced the table for the rest of my parents' lives.

When Mother arranged bouquets, she'd step back
and sometimes say his name from memory—

his Blackness softly implied.

ANOTHER LETTER ABOUT THE WEATHER

You still send letters though you are dead
and because you are free of the US Postal Service
they arrive anytime—
in the car at a light as a mother
grabs her wound-up children from the street,
in the middle of Australian costume dramas,
or while I forage in the pantry,
famished and not even hungry.

Here's one now, praising me
for the little songs I made up on the piano,
my lavishly romantic valentines, and recalling
our annual excursion to the dog show
where once you let me buy a Twinkie
and we impersonated for each other
elaborately ponytailed and pompommed
groomers.

And every morning a letter arrives,
smelling of coffee and bacon and plans for the day,
describing the clouds as you always did,
but now from the other side.

THE LINGERIE CHEST

It was taller than I was—a tower. In the top drawers
out of reach and sight, handkerchiefs I never used
and dress gloves—accessories for an older girl of a
previous era.

In descending order: swimsuits and swim caps.
Nightgowns. Slips. White cable-knit knee-highs and
colored tights.

The middle drawer opened on utilitarian cotton briefs
stacked ten days deep. Their sizes were expressed as
years: 6 years, 10 years, I especially remember 12
years. They were worn, washed, then reappeared.
None of my wondering was spoken.

The lingerie chest was the only fine piece of furniture
in my room, pale and French between the bricks-and-
boards bookcase and tippy wicker table. I opened and
opened its drawers with their clattering brass pulls,
which describes the passing of my childhood,

alert for sudden lace or silk, for pink sensation. For
beauty. As if growing up could be effortless—in our
house, where I'd been given no names for any of this
and the words I didn't know were impossible to say.
The implications of a word like *lingerie.*

MAIDEN LADIES

They were plentiful back then—
black-hatted in museums of natural history,
staring into yellowed dioramas of basilisks,
swaying so as not to be confused for displays.

They paid their dimes on rainy afternoons
to sit with ten-year-old boys watching films
about Brazilian snakes and Madagascan bats
and could be counted on

to inform shop clerks of shameful declines
in quality, to order special extra-plain
undergarments, unappetizing cuts of meat,
and okra tablets. To jam their feet

into witches' shoes that made their ankles swell.
Then hats went out of style. Shop clerks
started talking back and the maiden ladies died.
They're not even in museums.

READING ALOUD

When young Arthur
on a mission for his older brother
assayed the sword in the stone
then advanced through a heavy hail
of wherefores and withals
to mount the anvil and grip the hilt
unheralded and alone,

my second son dismounted
from his spaceship bed,
approached the center
of their messy room
and in his red plaid pajamas
reached forth into the seamless air
and pulled.

HELICOPTER, CHERNOBYL

https://youtu.be/zuNtgYtF4FI

A blade in slow motion
      strikes a construction crane—
reminding me they're called *birds:*

the copter stills, tilts, drops
      like a shot bird,
dragging a bucket of sand for the meltdown.

I rerun the 21-second film.
      When its blade strikes a crane
the helicopter stalls, unsure

how to exit the scene.
      (Belly up, crumpling.)
The blade strikes a crane

and the bird descends out of eyeshot,
      crashing off-screen.
What exactly am I feeling?

So I repeat it. It's a fly brushed
      from the face of God,
in the face of what can't be contained.

A blade strikes the crane;
      the bird's descent
is another melting and becomes

Winslow Homer's painting of ducks
      stilled in flight by a hunter's gun—

except it's radiation.

Or was it just snow on my TV that April,
        enveloping the pilot
and a map of Europe?

What was happening to us all?
        Not yet certain
what I was seeing, watching a bird—

or was it a sky—fall.

THE MAN WHO PLAYED TOO MUCH TETRIS

It wasn't just the way he ate his toast
                                changed lanes
                                        or squeezed between
                                                two women
                                                on the elevator
He looked too often toward the sky
                        and talked too much
                                        with his hands
At meetings
            the space between executive heads
                                asked to be filled
                                        with the world
                                                caving in
At lunch
        birds swooped down
                    on his crumbs
                            the way he'd trained them

He was a doomsday prophet

He was up to his eyeballs
                flooded
                    with everything fallen
                                or falling
                                and try as he might
                                he couldn't
                                find space
                                for it
                                all

It made him sad
                    when the women stepped away

THE '90S

The Best Decade Ever? —New York Times

We remodeled a house the shape of a world war. Tore away
the McCarthyism and curse words in the basement. Repealed
the breezeway like an amendment to the Constitution.

We carpeted the civil defense bomb-shelter tile, replaced
the Monitor-and-Merrimack furnace, painted over the state
institutional pink and dirty green of dead presidents.

We dug out boxes of torn tweed coats, worn to hotels with
brass registers and bellboys that burned to the ground before
we were born. And dresses with secret stitchings, ancient
Kleenex balled in their sleeves and in their pockets rancid
lipsticks in gold-metal tubes. Then hauled them away

to make a house for ourselves, a shelter from the past,
an Ernst Hardware showcase for our valuables—modem
jacks, imitation Chihuly glass, Costco boxes. We swept
away the planting and picking, the prayers poking up like
rusty mattress springs, the ragamuffin children running
down the road. Our new appliances didn't speak or we
didn't listen.

POEM ENDING WITH LINES FROM
A CHARLIE BROWN CHRISTMAS

I enter my childhood home a newly minted
40-year-old orphan, desiring everything—

rifling through the kitchen junk drawer,
and the auxiliary rubber-band drawer

and the third drawer full of twist ties
and Styrofoam meat trays. I want like a robber

the silverware and the encyclopedia set.
I want my mother's sense of her own beauty.

I want the sound of the house
settling at night. I'm the baby of the family—

I want my brothers to love me more than I deserve.
I'm taking the sugar and creamer engraved

with Shakespeare: "To thine own self be true"
and "Actions speak louder than words."

I want the prizes at the bottom
of every box of cereal ever eaten here.

Before we sell the house with its dear ghosts
and take our turn growing old, I insist

on one last game of Risk and this time
I will not cry and will demonstrate strategy.

All I want is what I have coming to me.
All I want is my fair share.

WAKING UP STRANGE

Don't sleep in a parked car.
You wake, windows fogged, hands on the wheel,
the dash and controls suddenly foreign,

like a safe word repeated too often. What queer
drives brought you here? You hurtle ahead but the car
is still. You wake up turning the wheel

and avoiding its meaning. Turning a pink plastic wheel.
Pounding a rubber clown horn like a little girl. And harbor strange
fears of waking up driving. Of waking up lost. You wake in a car

and can't find your car. Turn the wheel and it locks. You're an alien.

PILLOW TALK

1

Of all their not-talking, mornings are their favorite.
He hears her eyelids flutter, she feels his long limbs still

and the exchange of atoms which is the feature
of old married couples, the continuity of years,

rolling landscape, and a sky too large to face.
"What did you dream?" he doesn't ask,

and she doesn't answer about the attic shops,
the basement portal into an unfamiliar backyard.

Every night they spend side by side, wading
through their private sleep symbols, their x's and o's.

One rises first and their separate lives begin
in independent three-point planes.

On their best days they intersect. Some mornings
she feels him washed up on her beach, not saying anything.

2

The spring she moved in
she was too old really, 25, to be the innocent

soaking her pillow with tears, homesick for her parents
and the town she left behind. But that's what he got.

They slept in sheets of bright Marimekko buds
on single stems, his feet hanging off the edge

of her double bed, his first pair of dress shoes in the closet.
She was crying like he'd done something wrong.

3

What he didn't say while she explained about the baby
coming. What he didn't say while the baby

was being born. While he cradled him along the length
of his forearm. While the baby took a first few steps,

little hands held high for balance.

4

Beside her in the car, steering them home. She keeps jerking awake,
thinking they'll crash, but his eyes are open.

5

He called an ambulance that December night
because she begged him to. He was calm. And led the strangers

into their bedroom, interpreting her turtle posture
for their uniformed guests. He trailed

the ambulance, parting the striped dark and silence
in their car. He sat beside her in the emergency room

and waited there when they wheeled her away
to perform experiments on her middle-aged body.

He drove her home in her nightgown.
Then they changed and went straight to work.

Much will be asked of us before this life is over.

6

The sound of him turning a page became the sound
of pressing a button and the sound of his breathing

became more pronounced, trudging up a steeper
and steeper hill, shouldering a backpack full of rocks.

7

The TV blaring downstairs, laughter, refrigerator opening
and closing, bare feet up the stairs and into the lit hallway.

A voice calls softly through their closed door
as though they were one person.

LET ME SLEEP 20 MORE MINUETS

—*note from Elisabeth, age 12*

Here's more buckles and silk ruffles, twenty
more waltzes and gavottes, twenty minutes
of intricately tatted footsteps

across a ballroom of god rays. Step
lighter than a shed eyelash, than twenty
slow breaths as Morning

(old schoolmarm) taps her baton. More minutes,
more spherical music, more slipper-steps
in high tops, Elisabeth. Here, my dear, twenty-

times-twenty minuets. Step, curtsy, it's over like that.

MY FATHER'S WATCH

The crystal shattered
while he wore it.

The hour, minute,
and sweeping second hands

flew into the weeds
beside the road.

Though it's buried
with him,

his watch's naked face
sometimes appears to me

like a moon.
Then Dad must cross

again
against the signal

on one more walk
to Mother's grave.

I flinch into
the star-shaped headlights,

hold on
until the watch-face moon

cracks up.

INTIMACY

You only get this haircut
from the barber who sleeps with you.

It's the endless attention to your ears
and eyebrows. It's the wrestling moves.

I wield shears, talk brusquely
with my hands, cut off your curls

with your head braced between my breasts
as you sit almost calmly.

Your bald spot is the view
from a glass-bottom boat. No sign of me

down there. Once on a beach vacation
you and I watched a wife with scissors

move across her husband's scalp
in a sarong. It ought to have been private

the way she shaved his neck and sideburns.
If I pinch with the electric razor

or pull your hair, you'll grab my wrist
and tear the tablecloth off your shoulders.

If I'm careful, you'll accept your haircut
with a nod.

This is intimacy. What was I pining for?

SPRING

I've walked in and out of elegant shops
all afternoon in a spring-green coat,

but nothing calls to me
except one camisole that costs more

than I make in a week.
I wander among customers, clerks,

and maybe gifted lovers, some young enough
to be my children. How will it be

never to know what the world withheld,
the ending not in sight though maybe

it's hiding in the dressing room while I
trail fingers on the pretty merchandise.

Something's at work when I stand in a doorway
weighing whether or not to go in—

the possibility that I'll pay everything
for what I find inside.

THIMBLEBERRY

One taste

and the rest
is what came after.
Little berry,

you're the flavor
of my best,
most necessary

kiss. Fit
for a tongue tip,
exactly.

You were nothing
until I picked
you once.

How long
do we willingly
live without?

How hungry
would I be if
I'd kept walking?

COMPARE THE MOVEMENT OF SWALLOWS

with Magritte's matrix of businessmen
carefully spaced and hovering in the sky
who move not at all

but might—a characteristic of swallows
ready to swoop or suddenly plummet,

though this is also nothing like Magritte's men
suspended in middle age
who may drop like leaky helium balloons
or escape into the vanishing point
but will not acknowledge how desperate you are
for something to happen.

And by "you" I mean me,
framed in a doorway
Magritte repeatedly painted empty.

The swallows last evening
dragged behind them my meanings
with hooks that hurt even in recollection,
a tug I can only describe as my life.

Magritte's men are unfastened from the air,
poised to rise or fall or disappear
if they'd just decide,

and by "men" I've meant all along
my husband in the yard
where he fails to hear me calling

or hears me and stands facing away,
utterly still.

HORSE LATITUDES

A raft of debris as large as Africa
accumulates in the Pacific gyre—

trash, plastic, rope, netting—a synthetic sea
of flotsam that will outlive us all.

Few ships enter. A windless ocean
strikes terror in the crew.

If you can't imagine
the camera pulling back, pulling back

until we see the curve of the earth,
pulling back to reveal the atmosphere's

blue glow and still not bounding
the garbage—if we can't acknowledge

the damage done—then recall your secret hurt
that churns and churns and won't

diminish—a spiral so huge,
your mind mutinies and denies it all.

THE FUKUSHIMA 50

"In fact there were never 50 of them. Hundreds of workers stayed at the plant, braving high levels of radiation to bring the reactors under control. Many are still there today." —BBC

"They are not heroes for us." —Fukushima survivor

In fact there were five who remained
each too ancient and repentant to be killed by radiation

The first suffered an ocean of cold   dark   and wet
without complaint

They lived and toiled on one biscuit baked into stone
one sip of water each   in oven temperatures   renouncing sleep

The second built a moat of ice
to contain the radiation

They worked unseen
while the rest of us camped on gym floors
and dreamed
                    eyes fluttering   emitting whines
                    while our feet twitched as if running
                    through poisoned orchards

The third plucked every green thing
and blew it clean before replanting it

We turned our backs on the Daiichi plant
to watch our laundry on the line decay

The fourth collected sickness in his pockets

We read the dangerous grass
like the wet tip of an official's pen
and waited for an explanation

The fifth built a temple
out of our shunning

ALL UNKNOWNS WERE EQUAL

when my head was still soft
like a mushroom

and I'd wake in the banded light
to a consciousness like moss.

How large that yellow-green world
with its shadow prints on the window,

but also the marshland that was *I*.
Some scale measured the two equal,

and since I could wander only a few steps
in either direction, I wasn't afraid.

This seems now like the vestigial memory
of some other, ancestral being,

though I still feel the blue satin quilt
pulled to my chin and watch myself

unfolding fingers from a hand
at the far reach of my arm

with a patience I'll never recover
or comprehend—

the patience of a low place in the land
waiting to become a sea

or maybe an inlet, since the self is rinsed
each day in the world.

Mother used to say
I'd lie quietly in my crib a long while.

for Jim Deatherage

SEVEN SEAS

The one we've fished to death,
that tosses ships till they sink,
so deep the fish at the fissures
squiggle instead of swim, glow
instead of gaze.

The one inside a conch shell
that sweeps us from the couch
to its shore—our first metaphor.

The sea of ones and zeros
with tributaries pressing <u>Send</u>,
where our secrets glitter
in the data gyre.

The sea of refugees, turned away, turned away, turned away,
crashing the razor-wire fence.

The sea of cash, thick
with trawlers' tangling nets, green
with the drowned and drowning.

The sea of regret
that surges and retreats
and sucks at our feet,
a tide that takes us nowhere.

And the final sea of liquid light
we'll only know from below.

OPERATION CROSSROADS

In July 1946, two atomic blasts were conducted by the US military at Bikini Atoll to study the effect of nuclear weapons on warships.

Sailors boarded the floating, abandoned ship—
a frigate about to become an ark—
unloading caged rats and mice, bags
of insect-laced meal, goats, and pigs,
which the men dressed in naval uniforms
of uncertain rank. They rubbed flash creams
into the shoats' whiskery skin,
shaved goats' hair in human styles,
which encouraged the willies and rude remarks.
Many were farm boys, checking rats
against a master list, sweat rolling down
their bare backs. They secured
goats in the galley, mice in the brig,
carried in cages or pulled by the neck.
The pigs in sick bay roamed among
the berths. They'd got their sea legs.
Two sailors pulled a hat on a pig
on deck but he wouldn't have it,
kept wriggling free, sensing their ridicule
or perhaps the despair underneath.
The pig they locked in a ship's head squealed
the minute the door clicked shut.
Sailors tied goats to bunks, to valves
in the engine rooms, backing out
of each tableau, closing hatches
on the bleating and shitting—
every animal anxious, picking up
on the sailors' cues. Then they debarked,
counting human heads three times

before pushing off, motored back
to the USS Burleson and moped
around the empty pens full of straw
where the pigs and goats had lived
on the high seas for a month.
The countdown began. Anybody
who bet on the pigs to live
lost, if not the day of the test then in a week
or in the second, undersea blast,
and had to pay up for his optimism—
except Pig 311, locked in the ship's head,
who was found later dog-paddling with sea turtles
toward Bikini Atoll.

GEORGE C. MARSHALL (AUTHOR OF THE MARSHALL PLAN)'S LEFT EAR

In childhood in the half light
of my door ajar

the general's portrait on my bedroom wall glowed
and his left ear grew

by borrowing light from a white stripe
in the American flag behind him

transforming it into a kind of receiver
or spying device

that tapped my dreams.
So I was afraid

but my father hesitated
to take the picture down explaining

it had to do with saving Europe
after the war.

This is what I understood: my fear
budging against my father's love

for a man who merged at night
with the stars and stripes—

something to do with allegiance
something to do with light and dark.

2008

One night I dreamed Obama was stirring the coals of my dwindling campfire. We were alone. Blue tendrils of smoke punctuated the Mesozoic haze like a scene from *Jonny Quest*. Up and down the basin Americans smoldered. The tent flap behind us fell open meaningfully. His hand rested on my knee. My voice was low—I'm unnerved now by what I confided. We camped at the edge of a rain forest that hissed like a plane crash, like the mouth of a beast. Tangled and treacherous. Our ways on the eve of battle—tender and lit from within. *This is the last time*, I whispered. *I can't keep caring like this.*

HOSPITALITY

Caroline says, Refugees always tell me first
about the home they had before.

The one they ran from. That's gone now.

> *We had seven rooms and a terrace.*
> *Jasmine crowded our door.*

> *Our table had a view of the city.*
> *The river. An apricot tree.*

> *The sun shone in our windows early*
> *and woke us before the alarm.*

Caroline says, I look in the direction

their words are pointing so they know
I see it too. I tell them *It sounds beautiful,*

so they know I know this makeshift shelter
built of cardboard or plastic sheets or bamboo

is not their destiny. Their destiny has a roof
and a copper pot steaming on the stove

and a rose in a vase on a tray with cups of tea.

o o

Humiliation was the first Arabic word I learned,
Caroline says. To run from their homes

and schools and tree-lined boulevards,
barbershops and cafés, the hospitals

where their babies had been born;
to walk in the heat and dust for days, for weeks,

with blisters, crying, and a stream of grief;
to ride the highways and stop at checkpoints

where young boys pointed with their guns;
to arrive en masse at a makeshift camp and fight

to find a neck-high palm tree beside the road
providing a poor excuse for shade

and claim it; to make do for one night
wearing into how many more;

refugees can overcome, Caroline says.
But to be unable to offer a visitor tea?

It strips them down to nothing.

o o

It was Ramadan, Caroline says,
and this mother was young, 26 or 27,

with children popping in and out of her skirts
and arms.   She wanted so much

to offer me something, she literally reached
again and again for what wasn't there—

a tray of coffee and cups. A figment
I could picture just beyond her hands.

We walked out into the sunlight to say goodbye
and she spotted a tiny yellow flower—

the only growing thing I'd seen in camp that day.
She plucked it up saying, *Please take it. Please.*

This is what it means to be Syrian.

o o

I grew up an Army brat, Caroline says.
We moved state to state to these snoozeville towns.

My parents were tough and pulled themselves
out of poverty. I felt a poverty of another kind.

On 9-11, I watched all of it like a movie.
All day, wanting to see and taste it, to be there,

ash falling on my shoulders so I could understand.
I'm drawn to people by their shades of gray

when everything else has been taken;
how desperate they are to be seen.

Caroline says, I see them.

o o

I sometimes still dream of Afifa, Caroline says.
She taught teachers in Afghanistan.

Afifa wore the burka and I only knew her
by her voice, which was hilarious, the voice

of a comedienne. We set out on foot
one first day of school, passing men

as we headed out alone. She and I
were chatting together in our usual way

when Afifa pulled back her burka
and a woman appeared, entirely different

than the one I knew—much older, gray,
with worry lines—but I recognized

that grin from her voice. She posed,
back against a tree, like a model,

so I would take her picture on my phone.
When I get anxious sometimes

I look at the picture and think of her,
still in Afghanistan, say some Saturday night

back in Chicago when I'm in line at a comedy club.
You can't let the guilt get to you.

I know Afifa would want me to enjoy the show.
She'd go too, if she could.

o o

Caroline says, You would recognize the sound
of chatter in the Iraqi camps—

the call and response of mothers and children,
family squabbles, grocery lists written in the air.

But an eerie quiet settles on the Rohingyan camps
in Bangladesh. They've escaped, but brutality

is a sickness the Rohingya can't shake.
They live in perpetual limbo with no idea

of what's to come. I interviewed one refugee
whose answers were so brief and unadorned,

it felt like a listless game of ping-pong.
She described running from their burning village

and her sister, forced to stop mid-escape
to deliver her imminent child.

And while she told this story, another woman
nursed an infant, listening a little,

but only a little. This was the very sister
who birthed her baby on the road,

in a makeshift delivery room with sky for a ceiling
and tarps for walls held up by her family

to preserve what dignity they could.
The only thing the sister would say was *Shameful.*

o o

At dusk the Rohingyan camps find an evening rhythm,
Caroline says. The women and children

retreat into bedtime but the men linger
until the beautiful call to prayer echoes

from the makeshift mosque. Behind it,
the low grind of tractors building roads

for the thousands of new arrivals.
Last June it was a bamboo forest without interruption.

By October, Caroline says, not a tree in sight.
Clusters of bamboo huts and the quiet voices

of mothers and fathers and grandparents and children.
The smell of lentils cooking.

o o

Caroline says, In Haiti after the earthquake,
thousands of homeless took possession

of a golf course which became an endless camp
in every direction including time.

At night though, after meals and chores
and putting down the children, a woman's voice rose

out of the maze of the anonymous. A woman sang
a lullaby to her babies so beautiful and large

it became a lullaby for everyone who heard it—
for the tens of thousands who ached for sleep

and pleasant dreams,
a twilight descant over the tent tops.

o o

Caroline says, I was walking in the heat
through a new camp outside Mosul

when Chris beside me heard his name
called by his old interpreter from years ago.

Now Petrus was a displaced person.
Come see my wife! he invited from his short palm tree,

and we sat down with his gathered family.
They showed us videos on their cell phones

of their home and escape, asking us please
to tell the world. And while we listened,

out came a tray of hot tea in glass cups.
Where had this come from?

Had it arrived from some previous,
still-coherent life? Another family probably,

several palm trees over, who had seen
the critical need for immediate hospitality—

steaming cups of tea with sugar
in 110 degree heat in the nonexistent shade.

We were welcomed, Caroline says.

for Caroline Brennan

WITH SEAGULLS

The wind today contains some errant sea breeze,
redolent of the fifth day of our honeymoon
when we bought a pail and shovel

at a hardware store.
I'm pondering the sci-fi novel you described
over fish and chips barely mentioning

the characters, since love
and human frailty are secondary
to black hole transport and the problems

of colonizing the ring around a moon.
Then you segued to the data center at work
and my mind defragged for a while.

In one of the chambers of your heart
a seagull is always riding a thermal,
genius of the physics of the wing.

In my family growing up, seagulls
were considered rude opportunists
with vacant looks and dirty minds.

I forget for years at a time
how far you and I have traveled,
then a seagull drops down for a French fry

and there you are, holding so still,
the transaction between you is personal,
and delicate, like when two married people
start liking each other again.

EMERGING FIGURE

I

It's a man
wobbling
onto the highway
centerline

out of the almost
dark and into my
high beams

like a cursor
blinking
onto
a blank screen
         but a man

in the nearly-
winter night

○ ○

My hair
stands with him

on end

I slam the
brakes
swerving and
frantic he's chosen
for both of us

Flinch
so I can't
see

o   o

Then an atomized
line
dashes
behind me

a glow
in the rearview
mirror

as headlights
puncture my
windshield
strike and keep
striking

2

I didn't choose this romance.
What does it mean that he chose me?

I wander the house months later,
turning out lights.

The man on the highway
bobbles again in the closing
distance, deciding if I will strike.

Grip tight, breath
fluttering up the flag pole—

a desperate stretch of desert
penetrates me.

3

On a highway

        following a river

      shaped by a canyon   carved   by ancient cataclysmic floods

         in a canyon

           shaped by a river

              rushing 15,000 years toward its mouth

     you walk out from a curtain of trees

         and what if I'd blinked twice

         or changed the station?

○ ○

I wake   blinking you away

    See how you carve my sleep

        into shavings?   See how I'm

           worn down?

        Here comes another wave

              flooding my right mind

o o

You mount the centerline

        missing your antlers

Apple trees
crowd the shoulder
        picked of all but a few   soft remains

The only radio station

        spins 70s hits

        Time keeps on slippin', slippin', slippin'

            outrunning my headlights

o o

The country ahead
        teeters
          under a smatter   of stars

    My dashboard   conjures
        a space capsule

I hurtle into

                                               the dark

     pinned

          by speed

          and helplessness

          by what I see   and can't   stop

LILACS

As though we could string pearls into a necklace

of only good moments, between knots of waxed

string. Tonight, a month after the last lilac bloomed,

I finally noticed, and no hothouse could make the bushes

flower again late, early, whatever you call the period

after you've lost everything. Still, cells replicate,

shed skin is replaced. We are not who we were.

I'd seen the lilacs, gone through the motions

of breathing in, swirled the scent in the goblet

of my brain but I wasn't listening until

this evening, after the first warm day in June

when I considered how fine a bunch of lilacs

would be, enough to fill my arms, to hide my face

in their tender, sweet nostalgia for ordinary life.

ACKNOWLEDGMENTS

Thanks to Tavern Books for permission to publish the epigraph, from *Duino Elegies* by Rainer Maria Rilke, translated by Gary Miranda.

Thanks to Farrar, Straus and Giroux for permission to republish, in "Letter to Rilke," excerpts from "The Fifth Elegy," "The Seventh Elegy," and "The Tenth Elegy" from *Duino Elegies*, bilingual edition, by Rainer Maria Rilke. Translation copyright © 2000 by Edward Snow. Reprinted by permission of North Point Press, a division of Farrar, Straus and Giroux.

Thanks to the editors of the following publications where these poems originally appeared, sometimes in other versions:

"Instead of Sheep," *[PANK]*; "To Dotted Lines," *The Adroit Journal*; "On This Day in History," *Crab Creek Review*; "Street Scene, 1964," "Our Fathers," "Helicopter, Chernobyl," *Poetry Northwest*; "Married Love," *Connotation Press*; "Story That Won't End Well," *Whole Terrain Journal*; "A Child's Book of America," *Moss*; "1968" (as "Coconut") and "Intimacy" (as "You only get this haircut"), *Word Riot*; "Estranged" and "Spring," *Southern Poetry Review*; "Andy Warhol, 1986," "A Childhood Fear of Georges Braque," "The Lingerie Chest," and "The Fukushima 50," *Sierra Nevada Review*; "Another Letter about the Weather," "Reading Aloud," and "All unknowns were equal," *Stringtown*; "Maiden Ladies," *The Iowa Review*; "The Man Who Played Too Much Tetris," *Reimagining Place*; "Poem Ending with Lines from A Charlie Brown Christmas," *New Letters*; "Waking Up Strange" and "Seven Seas," *Tar River Poetry*; "Let me sleep 20 more minuets," *The Monarch Review*; "Thimbleberry," *Orion*; "Compare the movement of swallows" and "2008" (as "I Dreamed of Obama on the Night of His First Election"), *Plume*; "Horse Latitudes," *Third Coast*; "Lilacs," *Cascadia Review*.

Thanks to the editors of the following anthologies and websites where some of these poems were republished:

"To Dotted Lines" in *Fire on Her Tongue* by Two Sylvias Press; "Our Fathers" and "Seven Seas" on the *Verse Daily* website; "Another Letter about the Weather" in the online anthology *All We Can Hold*; "Reading Aloud" in *All We Can Hold* by Sage Hill Press; "Helicopter, Chernobyl" on *The Daily Vandal* website; "Waking Up Strange" on *The Seattle Review of Books* website; "Horse Latitudes" in *The Pushcart Prize XXXVI: Best of the Small Presses*; "Lilacs" in the *Get Lit! Twentieth Anniversary Anthology*.

Thanks to Jim Jones for reproducing "Let me sleep 20 more minuets" as a letterpress postcard.

I am grateful to Caroline Brennan for her time with me and for her inspiring work. Thanks to Mona O'Loideain Rochelle for commissioning an earlier version of "Hospitality" for an evening to benefit Catholic Relief Services, and to Sam Green.

Thanks to Humanities Washington for commissioning the poem "Night Train to Salzburg" for Bedtime Stories.

My thanks to Artist Trust for a GAP Award and to King County 4Culture for an arts grant at precisely the moments their encouragement felt crucial, to Bloedel Reserve and Hedgebrook for the gift of time and beauty that will remain with me always, and to Jack Straw and the Washington State Poet Laureate program for expanding my boundaries.

I am indebted to my first readers and writing companions who were essential as I struggled to see and revise this collection. Heartfelt thanks to Dianne Aprile, Elizabeth Austen, Tarisa Ball, Sharon Bryan, T. Clear, Leanne Dunic, Holly J. Hughes, Kathryn Hunt, Tim Kelly, Jared Leising, Erin Malone, Anne McDuffie, Ted McMahon, Donald Mitchell, Rosanne Olson, Peter Pereira, Sylvia Pollack, Spencer Reece, Susan Rich, Martha

Silano, Megan Snyder-Camp, Jeanine Walker, Katharine Whitcomb. One more time—Sharon Bryan.

Many thanks to Linda Bierds for insights that made this a better book and to the excellent University of Washington Press.

Thank you, Steve.

ABOUT THE AUTHOR

ELISABETH FLENNIKEN

Kathleen Flenniken is the author of two previous poetry collections: *Famous* (University of Nebraska Press, 2006), named a Notable Book by the American Library Association, and *Plume* (University of Washington Press, 2012), a finalist for the William Carlos Williams Award. Her poems have appeared in *Poetry Northwest, [PANK], The Iowa Review, Orion,* and *Third Coast.* Her awards include fellowships from the National Endowment for the Arts and Artist Trust, a Pushcart Prize, the Prairie Schooner Book Prize in Poetry, and a Washington State Book Award. She served as Washington State Poet Laureate from 2012 to 2014.